Book

of

Mercies

Book of Mercies

By GEORGE ARTHUR FRANTZ

"Let thy mercies come also unto me, O Lord."
—Psalm 119:41

THE BOBBS-MERRILL COMPANY, INC.
INDIANAPOLIS · *Publishers* · NEW YORK

The New Testament quotations in this publication are from the *Revised Standard Version of the New Testament,* copyrighted 1946 by the Division of Christian Education, National Council of Churches, and used by permission.

The Old Testament quotations are from the *King James Version.*

The three lines of poetry on page 61 are from Robert Browning's "The Ring and the Book."

The Negro work song on page 105 is from *The British Weekly.*

The five lines of poetry on page 108 are from Robert Browning's "Paracelsus."

The six lines of poetry on page 119 are from Francis Thompson's "The Hound of Heaven."

"A Prayer for Our World" was suggested by a prayer which was published in *The Expository Times.*

COME INTO THE
HIGH PLACES

IT IS THE *Grand Central Station in New York on a sticky, sultry August afternoon.* Suddenly the walls around you take voice and speak. "Train for ——." *In twenty minutes a train is starting for the Adirondack Mountains. Men and women and children are sitting all around you in the waiting room, listening eagerly to what the walls are saying. For they are taking that train.*

"Train for Lake George." *And you can feel in the words the healing coolness of the winds of God as they blow across the lake. The sights of the city are lost and you are looking on the "sunset touch" in sky and water. Indeed, "There's enough for fifty hopes and fears as new and old at once as Nature's self." For a space of time the din of the city dies away and you are in the silence of the woods at night. No glare of street lamp blinds you to the heavenly light. No honk of horn disturbs your thought. The quiet of God rings you round, and you hear a voice of stillness which the roar of the city all too easily drowns. And there is the first flush of the summer dawn; the many-throated rapture of the birds as they sing their thanks to God for the victory of light over darkness, and begin a new day with praise.*

Thinking of it all for a few minutes brings peace. But

5

what will it not mean to those who are taking the train? They will live for days and nights in the refreshment you only imagine.

This book is a voice which speaks to you of a journey into the country of God. Many around you are taking the trip. It recalls your mind to the peace and joy of your fellowship with Him.

Come into the High Places. There are Houses of God open all the year round.

The Way

of

Thanks

The Way of Thanks

"GRATITUDE is the memory of the heart." This is what a child in a deaf-and-dumb school wrote in answer to the question, "What is gratitude?" This child's heart was neither deaf nor dumb. With our two good ears and tongues for many words, we are shamed by the handicapped child.

Frances Havergal, whose hymns we sing, kept a *Journal of Mercies*. The way of thanks is the "King's Highway." Our Lord Jesus Christ used that road. Many of His prayers are thanksgivings.

The way of thanks leads out of the land of complaining into the place of music and of song.

It is the way out of self-centered thoughts into thoughts of God. *They shall abundantly utter the memory of thy great goodness, and shall sing.* (Psalm 145:7)

It is the way out of envy and covetousness. Thanks light up our little homes so warmly that we stop looking at our neighbor's big house and begin to enjoy our own.

The way of thanks is the way of peace and success in Christian living. The memory of what God has done for us in Christ is the motive and the power of our life in Him.

Happy is the man who keeps a book of mercies!

On Being Religious

THERE are only two ways of being religious. The one way is to try to put God in debt to us. We think that we can be such good people that God will then owe us something; and we can collect in the currency of peace of mind and even in pride over our superior moral attainments. This is the way of the Pharisee. Paul tried this way and found it bitterly disappointing. He discovered that he could not perfectly keep God's laws. The best he could do was not good enough. The end of this way is despair.

The other way of being religious is simply to acknowledge the greatness of our debt to God, because He so loved us that He gave His only son that we might be delivered from all our sins. We cannot earn the Peace of God, but we can receive it.

We cannot put God in debt to us, but we can gratefully acknowledge that we owe everything good to Him. This way lies the Peace that passes understanding. Our whole life is lived in the gladness of gratitude for a love so great that no one can earn it. Paul found this way, when Christ found him.

On Keeping Young

THE secret of keeping young is the willingness to grow old. If you want to appear old, then dress and try to act young. Age is as much a gift of God as is youth. Don't try to avoid it; welcome it. There is no hope of happiness in age if we think we are indispensable. Interests should increase though activities must decline. Age gives us opportunities to develop capacities and interests which the harsh pressures of earlier life left little time to cultivate.

We need not fear loneliness if we are friendly and are genuinely interested in people. The best insurance against a lonely old age is to make friends among the younger people; they will be here when your contemporaries are gone.

Bereavement will not be bitter if we learn to thank God for the love we have already received, and which is a part of our life forever.

The great blessing is a contented mind, thankful for all God's amazing mercies and eager to see those yet to come from His generous hand.

We are as young as our faith in God, and as old as our doubt of His love. We are as young as our love for people, and as old as our selfishness. We are as old as our despair of goodness, and as young as our hope in Christ.

Use
Your
Brains

JESUS said: *You shall love the Lord your God . . . with all your mind.* (Mark 12:30) Put some brainwork into your love. Our piety has no more right to be stupid than has science, or business, or statesmanship. We do not honor God with minds softened by sentimental laziness. A soft mind and a flabby body are both marks of misspent years.

The evils of the world are not all caused by malevolence; many of them come from stupid indolence. And much of our stupidity is not inborn; it is our own achievement. Some people think that there is no case for the Christian view of life, because they have never read one mind-stretching book on the side of the angels. Of books on the side of the demons they read many.

We often go haltingly on in the Christian way, when we could walk and run and leap, praising God, if we were willing to use our brains, and love God with our minds. *Therefore gird up your minds* and read a book that makes you hilarious with confidence in God. Love Him with your mind. You will enjoy it. You might start with *The Case for Christianity* by C. S. Lewis.

Be of Good Cheer

It is a glory of our Christian faith that it is a religion which makes sadness one of the deadly sins. Christ commands us to be of good cheer, and He gives us the joy He commands. He has put things right between God and us. And being right with God is the fountain of joy. He gives us power to live successfully, and there is joy in succeeding.

He has made us sure of God. Certitude about God has joy; doubt has none.

Joy is at once the right and duty of a Christian whose conscience and prayers are in good order.

It is our joy that attracts and wins those *having no hope and without God in the world.*

Five times in the Gospels our Lord Jesus says, *Be of good cheer.*

I have said this to you, that in me you may have peace. In the world you have tribulation; but be of good cheer, I have overcome the world. (John 16:33)

13

Our
Advocate

"I WANT a lawyer." So men say when they get into trouble. They want a counsel for their defense. The Bible tells us that this is a part of Christ's work for us. *I am writing this to you so that you may not sin; but if any one does sin, we have an advocate with the Father, Jesus Christ the righteous.* (I John 2:1)

He is our last line of defense, the final resource in every peril in our Christian life. The apostles speak of this work of Christ for us with a kind of adoring thankfulness. *Consequently he is able for all time to save those who draw near to God through him, since he always lives to make intercession for them.* (Hebrews 7:25)

He died for us, and by His death has dealt with our sin. He is clothed in His crimson robe when He represents our case before God.

Would you like to go into God's presence, unguided and on your responsibility, rather than with your hand in the hand of Christ, who knows your case and is worthy to plead for you? When we present our prayers in His name, He presents them again to God for us. And we rest our case in His hands.

Choosing Your Facts

WE ALL live in the same world, but as Plato said, "It is one kind of world to the man asleep, and it is another to the man awake." Traffic conditions required me one June day to fall in behind a garbage wagon. Believe me, it was a rotten world. And yet there were rose gardens at almost every house we passed, and there were the love and laughter of children.

And furthermore, there is a philosophy behind a garbage wagon if the driver is willing to think. That wagon is evidence of a civic conscience. It is the redolent proof that the community has a conscience against garbage dumps in back yards, and is blessedly prejudiced in favor of sewer systems.

Our world has both garbage wagons and rose gardens. A shallow pessimist sees only the wagon. A shallow optimist sees only the garden. It is the wisdom of the wise to see both, to see life steadily and see it whole.

Wherefore look at all the facts. When God made man, He put him in a garden, not behind a garbage wagon. Look at all the facts. The chessboard is black, but it is white also. It takes both black and white to make a chessboard. And if the world were all black, then where in the world did white come from?

When you puzzle over the problem of evil, puzzle a little over the problem of good. Where did evil come from? But then where did good come from? It will do you good to ponder that. And remember that an utterly bad world could not produce even a bad conscience which accuses badness and judges and condemns badness—conscience is the awareness of right.

God
Gives
Himself

A MISSIONARY in Iran was learning the language. One day he asked his native teacher to tell him a story. The teacher thought and then told this story:

The great and good Shah Abbas liked to mingle with his people in disguise. Once dressed as a poor man he visited the fireman who heated the water for the public baths. The Shah sat with him and they talked. When mealtime came the fireman shared his black bread and his jug of water with his new friend. The Shah came often. The fireman opened his heart to him, because he loved him.

One day the Shah told him who he really was. The fireman only looked at him in love and wonder. He asked nothing. The Shah asked, "Do you not understand, I can make you rich?"

The fireman replied, "Yes, my lord, I understand. You have left your palace to come to sit with me in this dark place. You have shared my coarse bread. You have listened to my thoughts. You care whether I am sad or glad. You can give me nothing greater, nothing richer. For others you may give riches, but to me you have given yourself. I ask only that you will never take your friendship from me."

Behold, I stand at the door and knock; if any one hears my voice and opens the door, I will come in to him and eat with him, and he with me. (Revelation 3:20)

A Message to Mother

Love for his mother set S. F. B. Morse to invent the telegraph. He went to Europe to study the art of painting. The door of his home had closed behind him. He had scarcely arrived in Europe when he began to realize that it would be months before his first letter could reach his parents; and he knew that his mother would be anxious about him; and he was already longing for word from her.

He wrote these words to her: "Three thousand miles are not passed over in an instant." Then he asked himself: "Why should they not be passed over in an instant?" Love for his mother set him to revolving the idea of quick communication; and he worked on it, till at last he gave to the anxious mothers of the world the means of learning how their faraway children are. He sent out his first message over the wire: "What hath God wrought!"

A son's love for his mother gave us the telegraph. It is still available for messages to mothers. The telephone came in due time. And prayer has always been a way of reaching mothers. We can send them messages through the heart of God, whenever we will. These messages do not lose in God's delivery of them.

No
Zero

THE Romans had no zero in their system of numbers; they had only whole numbers. They did not even consider zero as a number; yet they carried on a worldwide business; they had corporations and dividends; they had banks and interest.

God has no symbol for zero in His big business called Operation Mankind. *God so loved the world*—the whole world of people; and every person to Him is a whole person. He knows no fractions in people.

Jesus says that the shepherd had lost one sheep, not one per cent of his flock of a hundred. The woman had lost one coin, not ten per cent of her money. The father had lost one whole son, not fifty per cent of his boys.

God always has carried on His business with us without a symbol for zero, because we are never decimal fractions to Him; we are His children.

He loved me, and gave Himself for me.

The Passive Voice

WE LIKE THE ACTIVE. "Strenuous," "energetic," "striving," "go-getter," "peppy." Such words as these keep our sentences nervous.

Could this account for our lack of tranquility? We still seem to think that we have to earn our own salvation. We major on what we have to do. The New Testament glories in what God does for us.

All the significant verbs of the New Testament are in the passive: *You were redeemed. Unless one is born anew. You are saved. Among all those who are consecrated. Since we are justified by faith, we have peace with God through our Lord Jesus Christ.* We are kept by the power of God, and this is our peace.

We know that the love of God is doing for us what we cannot do for ourselves. Our energies, once squandered on trying to save ourselves, are now freed for living the life of gratitude in serving God's other children.

Discovering the passive is the Grammarian's Resurrection. *For by grace you have been saved through faith; and this is not your own doing, it is the gift of God—not because of works, lest any man should boast.* (Ephesians 1:8-9)

My
Necessary
Words

SHAKESPEARE found twenty-five thousand words necessary to speak the comedy, the tragedy and the history of our human life. Milton found twelve thousand sufficient to tell about our loss of Paradise and how it was regained for us by Christ.

The twenty-one volumes of my *Oxford English Dictionary* contain more than five hundred thousand words.

For me as a Christian there are two basic and absolutely necessary words. They are "Yes" and "No." I cannot even begin my life with Christ until I have learned to say "Yes" to Him. I cannot continue my life with Him without saying "No" to all the low whispers of the Tempter.

There is much interest in religion today, and many discussions about it, but how little commitment to Christ!

Learning to say "Yes" to Christ is the beginning of a Christian.

God's

Extras

Pools and the Sea

IN THE marshy ground by the sea's shore two kinds of pool are found. The one is full of stagnation and death. The other is clean with the salty tang of the ocean in it.

They are often found not far apart. After the rains they look much alike. But the sun beats down on them for a few days. The one slowly covers itself with a green scum. The other is perennially clean. What makes them so different? The secret is this—the one lies near enough to the ocean to be washed by its daily tides. Into it there sweeps twice in twenty-four hours the pure salt water from the deeps of the middle seas. This pool is in reality a part of the great waters. The other pool stands alone and receives its waters only from the corrupted streams of our soiled earth.

Two men live near together, in the same block. They work in the same building downtown. They have many friends in common. The sun of prosperity shines on them both. And a good friend who loves the two of them sees a subtle change come over the one. His life grows fevered and unwholesome. A scum forms over the once-fresh water. Some friends first feel a lack in him and then find excuse for absence.

The other man has the simple, wholesome tang of salt in him. Here the sun can breed no larvae of death. Death dies in these saline waters.

And you have run far ahead of me. You have long since finished the story for yourself. You have said: "Of course, of course, the one is swept by the tides of the life of God." Of course, of course.

23

The
Key

A SOBER and intelligent man stood before the door of his own house. The night was stormy and bitterly cold. There was warmth within. The key was in the mailbox, where every sensible key is kept.

He drew it out; fingered it; felt its queer notches and lined depressions. He knew it would open the door, because it had already opened the door for his family that night. It had opened that door for the people who lived in the house before him.

It will unlock it now if he will insert and turn it.

But suddenly he says to himself: "I will not. The key is such a queer thing, so arbitrary. Why does it need to be so fantastic in shape? Why this triangular point here, and this corrugation there?

"I never saw inside that lock. I don't know how it works. I am a man of reason. This thing is too mysterious for me to have anything to do with it. If I use this thing that I cannot see, some of my friends will call me superstitious."

And he stays out on the porch in the cold. Inside there is warmth.

The house is the House of Faith, warm with the love of the Father and rich in the service and fellowship of His other children. The key is the truth Christ put into our hands. The man—you know him, too.

Jesus says, *I will give you the keys of the kingdom of heaven.* (Matthew 16:19)

24

The Way

HIGHWAYS are not made to display engineering skill. A through street is opened because a crowd of people want to travel home at night. A road is for travel.

The early Christians showed their deep understanding of our faith. They called their new life in Christ "The Way." It is an open and much-traveled road. Many men and women have gone this way ahead of you. It is clearly marked. The Christian life can be lived.

It is a specific path through dangerous situations. It starts just where you stand now. Take the first turn to the right and then straight on. The road is finished. There are no detours. It leads straight on through the swamps of temptation. It is narrow here, but it is built up so no slime detains you. It runs right across the dark gulf called death, and souls pass over unafraid. This is "the new and living way" which Jesus has opened for us.

Other roads lead to the edge of the abyss and end. "Road closed." No, it is not "closed for repair." There is no road farther. "The road dies there," as men say up north.

Yonder is the way of the sensualist. That way leads to the grave. Lust and liquor die with death.

There is the way of worldly ambition and pride. The stuff of power and pride do not cross. They stay here.

There is the way of the careless. It is crowded with silly souls whose chief interest is an erotic novel, and a game. The sign to that road reads: *If you live according to the flesh you will die.* (Romans 8:13)

25

Point
of
No Return

"WHEN I crossed the Atlantic two years ago by clipper, we left New York bound for the Azores with a heavy load of gasoline in our tanks. We had enough gasoline on board so that if word of heavy weather should come to us even when we were well over a thousand miles at sea we could still turn back and reach New York safely. But on the pilot's charts in the instrument room there was a line drawn. It was called the point of no return. If we crossed that line we must make for the Azores whatever the weather might be. For now our supply of fuel could no longer take us back; now we must go on." So writes Douglas V. Steere.

There is a "point of no return" in the Christian's way, and until we have passed that point we are not really committed to Christ; we are not yet all out for Him. We have not yet believed that "God is able"; that He can send a tail wind to help the gasoline—the unseen to augment the seen.

In the Bible the word for wind and the word for spirit is the same word. God has committed Himself to raise a powerful wind for any soul that is committed to the Christian way.

And my God will supply every need of yours according to his riches in glory in Christ Jesus. (Philippians 4:19)

The Gate

AND *the twelve gates were twelve pearls, each of the gates made of a single pearl*. (Revelation 21:21)

The gates into the City of God's Peace are many, but they are all of one kind; each one is a pearl. Now of all jewels the pearl has the humblest origin. It is not created, like the diamond, in the fiery and fierce pressures of the depths of the earth.

The pearl is something compounded of a wound and the agony of a wound, and the resources of God for the healing of that agony, in a humble living thing.

This is our gate into God's Living Peace. We meet an intolerable hurt; we must have healing, and none but God can heal. We have been separated from one greatly beloved; we must know where and how God reunites us. We have sinned; we must have forgiveness. God alone can forgive sin. We have been defeated, and we know the bitterness of failure; we must know Christ who alone can make us more than conquerors.

Each of the gates made of a single pearl. Duke and dustman enter by the same gate, the gate of a great need, which God only can supply.

Power

THERE is power which can fill us with joy and peace, and cause us to overflow with hope. This power works in our joyless and drooping spirits. Power to be effective must belong to the realm in which it is to work.

We use the word *power* in different meanings. Language has its own poverty. We speak of a powerful telescope, and a powerful locomotive, and a powerful personality. But the powerful telescope cannot pull a train. The most powerful locomotive cannot pull the hopeless spirit out of me, nor draw out of my mind fearing thoughts.

The power which brings joy and peace into my heart is the power of a powerful personality. It is the power of the Holy Spirit. Physical forces cannot do spiritual work.

The power of the Holy Spirit is the power which dwelt in Jesus Christ. This is the power which made Him master of every temptation. It sustained Him on the cross. This is the power which raised Him from the dead and exalted Him to the place at God's right hand.

This is the power which changed Peter and Mary Magdalene and Paul. This is the power of the Living God working in us.

May the God of hope fill you with all joy and peace in believing, so that by the power of the Holy Spirit you may abound in hope. (Romans 15:13)

THE *fruit thereof shall be for meat, and the leaf thereof for medicine.* (Ezekiel 47:12)

Leaves

for

Healing

Health is one result of real religion, and it is important; but we must remember that the most important thing in life is our right relation with God. When we put health first, we are like a tree that runs to leaves; leaves are receiving the attention that belongs to fruit.

Neither must we forget that a tree has leaves. Faith in God does affect our physical health; trust in Christ cures worry and brings serenity. When we are so busy with Christ's work in the world that we have no time or mind for thinking up fancied pains, we are healthier people. When we love God with all our strength of body, we keep ourselves free from the self-indulgences which are the cause of much sickness.

When our spirits are receiving daily the abundance of life which Christ gives to us in our thanksgiving—from His Word and for His work—then we are delivered from our sense of inadequacy for our tasks, and we are able for everything through Christ who strengthens us.

A heart cleansed from pride and resentment and greed and impurity is a healed heart. Physical health is often a bonus from Heaven for work well done and for work yet to be done. *And the leaves of the tree were for the healing.* (Revelation 22:2)

God's
Bonus

GOD does not hold us at His minimum wage. He has many a bonus for us at the year's end and all through the year. Grace is the Bible's word for bonus.

Look at the flowers as an example. God might have propagated plants in some dull way. Instead, He threw in all the witchery and beauty of the book of spring, written in flowers, grace upon grace, spilled on us out of His generous hand.

Think of our children. God might have peopled the earth by some easy and dull way; but He chose the wonder of a little child, given to us in our love and creative will. He gave us the happy months lengthening out into years, when they are utterly dependent on our love and care.

Take for example the gift of His Good News in Christ. God might have published the Gospel by sky-writing, but He did not choose that way. He gives to us the joy of seeing the light come on faces dark with fears. *You shall be my witnesses. How beautiful are the feet of those who preach goodness.*

Look for God's extras. He gives them. *Blessed be the Lord, who daily loadeth us with benefits.* (Psalm 68:19)

Your Name Is Called

In the book of Isaiah we are told: *And I will give thee the treasures of darkness, and hidden riches of secret places, that thou mayest know that I, the Lord, which call thee by thy name, am the God of Israel.* (Isaiah 45:3)

Those called on to walk in the shadows of darkness and secret places, even temporarily, have many opportunities to attest the fulfillment of the Lord's promise.

One treasure of the shadows is Peace. This treasure alone is above price—yea, even though all the wealth of the world were offered in the market places for its purchase.

The shadow of Perfect Peace, God's gift to us through Christ, is more easily seen, more powerful than all other shadows. *Yea, though I walk through the valley of the shadow of death, I will fear no evil.*

The all-conquering love of Almighty God and the teachings of Christ are realities of today—not yesterday—which all of us can feel and touch. And it may be well to recall that in Isaiah we are told that the God of Israel calls us by name.

Blessed Be Hunger

WE ALL hunger and thirst. Appetite is clamorous. It must be satisfied or we perish. We cannot forget that we are hungry and thirsty.

Jesus says that we are happy when we have the appetite for goodness. There is no shortage in this commodity. Goodness is not rationed. God has ample stock for us. *Blessed are those who hunger and thirst for righteousness, for they shall be satisfied.* (Matthew 5:6)

What is our real need? Is it what we now desire? Or is our first need to be able to want what we ought to have?

Jesus came into this world to give us the appetite for righteousness; and righteousness is in being in right relationship with God and others.

When the desire for right relations is as persistent as appetite, and as demanding, we are well on the way toward being happy people. Desire and duty are now one. We are no longer a house divided against itself. "I want" and "I ought" speak with one voice. Our divided hearts are healed.

In the spiritual economy of God's Plenty our hunger is met with *bread and to spare.*

SALVATION is the whole process by which Christ rescues us from sin, brings us back home, and sets us to to work for Him.

See it in a picture: A house is burning. There is a violin in it, a Stradivarius. A music lover, knowing the danger of the destruction of the violin, rushes in, at great risk, and saves it. That is salvation.

But the violin was injured by the fire. The music lover takes it to an expert craftsman. He repairs it lovingly, for he knows its value. That also is salvation.

Now the violin is rescued from the fire; its injuries are repaired; its wounds are healed.

A great violinist takes it; tunes it; draws the bow over it; and it speaks to us. That also is salvation.

The complete salvation of the violin is its complete rescue, its complete repair, and its complete use.

Jesus Christ rescues me from danger; He restores my soul; He puts me to work.

And Jesus said to him, "Today salvation has come to this house, since he also is a son of Abraham. For the Son of man came to seek and to save that which was lost." (Luke 19:9-10)

Kingdom for the Poor

BORN to poverty, our Lord has a right to speak to the poor. The kingdom of the world is obviously for the rich. Pleasure and power are in possessions, so it seems. But this world's wealth often stands in the way of the Other World's blessing.

A man can be impoverished by his possessions. *How hard it will be for those who have riches to enter the Kingdom of God.* The rich can be saved, but they are saved not by means of riches, but in spite of them.

There is a power in wealth to hide needs which it cannot satisfy. The things that appear to fill life can empty it. The poor have this one less delusion to sweep away.

Poverty itself is not the passport to the Kingdom. The poor do not all possess this happy realm. It belongs only to the *poor in spirit,* to such as realize that they are weak, and ignorant, and sinful, and in utter need of God.

The man who knows that he is ignorant is already on the threshold of knowledge. The man who knows that neither possessions nor lack of possessions can make him happy is ready for God. And having God is having a Kingdom.

The *poor in spirit* know that life is not in things, but in God. Held by no thing we are God's possession.

The Meek Inherit

THE meek inherit the earth; they do not invade it. The earth is given to them by their Father; they do not have to grab at it.

Our real possessions are the things we are using as God means us to use them. In God's intention the right use of the earth is as a school for His children. Its real wealth is the wealth of the soul, and its most valuable product is character.

The true owners are right users. "All this is my land," said a man to his poor cousin. "Yes, but it is my landscape" was the gentle reply. When we see God's care in the lilies of the field and see that He notices a sparrow's fall, then we have an inheritance that no title deed can bestow.

The meek make no claim upon the earth except that it provide the place and the things in which they may become sons of God and brothers of men. And God will substantiate every such claim.

The meek obey God, and so become a terror to tyrannies. *Now the man Moses was very meek, above all the men which were upon the face of the earth* (Numbers 12:3), and his first recorded adult act was to kill a slave driver. The meek, asking of earth only a place in which to obey God, never assert themselves except in behalf of the oppressed. Meekness is the courage of the obedient.

Good
Judgment

Good judgment has a premium on it in our generation. An Air Force study of jet-plane crack-ups shows that seventy per cent of pilot errors can be traced to bad judgment compared with fifty per cent for propeller planes. This does not mean that jet pilots are deficient in judgment. It shows only how the speed of the jets puts judgment to a greater test.

The speed of a runaway wheelbarrow puts no great burden on a man's judgment. The speed of a runaway horse does not put much strain on him. A locomotive and a jet plane vastly increase that strain. The increase of the strain is as the square of the speed. And this is the world in which we live. The speed tests our judgment.

How do we get good judgment? Can we get enough to compensate for the increased speed?

Our Lord says, "My judgment is true." His judgment on war, and all social relations, on sex, and industry, on international affairs is true. We may have His judgment on all life. He will give us His mind and will and spirit; we may have His judgment for the asking. *O Lord . . . teach me thy judgments.* (Psalm 119:108)

He Humbled Himself

WHEN we humble ourselves, then no one can humiliate us. Humility cannot be humiliated. Humility is taking the lowest place; and when we have taken the lowest place, our next move can only be higher. Pride and arrogance can be humiliated.

Humility does not change the outside world. It is still a hard world, full of sin and suffering; but humility does change our attitude toward sin and suffering. Humility puts us among the neediest. We share their suffering, and because pride is gone from us we can help them.

This is why our Lord Jesus Christ was born in a stable. He took the lowest place, and He can lift us into the presence of God.

Have this mind among yourselves, which you have in Christ Jesus, who, though he was in the form of God, did not count equality with God a thing to be grasped, but emptied himself, taking the form of a servant, being born in the likeness of men. And being found in human form he humbled himself and became obedient unto death, even death on a cross. (Philippians 2:5-8)

Have this mind among yourselves, which you have in Christ Jesus. Having this mind in us is the true celebration of Christian days.

We Are
Never
Sorry:

For doing good to all,
For being patient with the ignorant,
For hearing before judging,
For thinking before speaking,
For holding an angry tongue,
For being kind toward the distressed,
For speaking evil of no one,
For stopping our ears to a talebearer,
For disbelieving many evil reports,
For praying for our enemies,
For serving Christ loyally,
For doing our duty,
For forgiving those who trespass against us,
For doing good without expecting a reward
These are blessings from the Lord, and they add no sorrow

Man's

Compassion

Begin with the Sky

WHEN the French painter Corot began one of his silver-gray landscapes, all tremulous with mist and sunlight, he always painted first the sky. He did this because it is the sky which gives the light and the color tone to the whole landscape.

We must begin with the sky. We look up to God because He gives the light and the color tone to life as we see it. The heavens give us perspective; we learn what is high and what is low, what is near and what is far.

We look at life in the light of heaven and we know that we are not merely creatures of economics, but that we have needs beyond bread. Our doctrine of God determines our view of what man is.

Begin with heaven, put the sky in our picture of life, and we have insight into human dignity and man's possibilities under God. We have roots in the earth, and we have hopes in heaven. Christ came from above to make us *servants of the Most High. Every good endowment and every perfect gift is from above.* (James 1:17)

The
Consolation
of God

Would it really console us if all our "whys" were answered? Why the child had to meet that deadly virus, and why he could not fight it off? Why the road was wet just then, and why you were on that curve at the fatal moment? If we had an answer, a scientific and philosophical explanation, for all our bruising questions, would that comfort us?

A child is not comforted by being told just why his toy broke, or why his finger hurts when it is pinched in the car door, or why his tummy aches. He is really comforted by feeling that his mother loves him, and that she can do something about it.

In this business of living we are all children with little minds and no very great wisdom. But God has gone to great trouble to assure us that He loves us; He has gone the length of Calvary. *In all their affliction he was afflicted, and the angel of his presence saved them: in his love and in his pity he redeemed them; and he bare them, and carried them all the days of old.* (Isaiah 63:9)

The great consolations are in love and in helping. There is love in this world. It comes to us in our need through friends and family. And this love is from God. This is the consolation of God. It is not chiefly in answering our "whys"; it is in answering our need for love.

Are the consolations of God small with thee? (Job 15:11)

Be Not Conformed

Any living thing that just fits its times is on the way out by extinction, or is on its way to become a parasite.

Several geologic ages ago—I think they say from the Lower Jurassic to the end of the Mesozoic—this world of ours saw a huge flying animal called a pterodactyl. The name means "wing-finger." He was a saurian, ornithosaur. He was so successful at flying that, when the climate changed and the vegetation changed with the climate, he could not find landing fields and he perished.

A queer little creature, feeble and without wings, except to his thoughts, survived and has put "old wing-finger's" bones in museums. Man has grown to be what he is by his struggle against bad times. And bad times are still our opportunity.

Our times are bad, so bad that we must see to it that all across the world there shall be places where brotherhood has built landing fields where our mechanical birds can come down, laden with good will for our brothers.

Monument to Joseph

A SMALL boy in a Sunday-school class listened to the story of the Prodigal Son, the story of a father's love and patience, and the liberty he gave to his son. The small boy then asked the teacher, "Are you sure God is like that?" His teacher answered, "Yes, God is like that. But why do you ask?" The boy replied, "Because my daddy is not like that."

Do you ever reverently visit that home in Nazareth where Jesus was a boy? Mary receives her honor, and she is worthy. There is a cult of Mary. In the light of all we know of the significance of a home for the child's sense of values and his idea of God, why is there no cult of Joseph?

In that home Jesus saw Joseph, lived with him, worked with him. The children went to him with their needs, their joys and their troubles. The boy Jesus saw a father, a good father, and in His talking to the people later He often pictures a good father, and then says, *How much more will your Father who is in heaven give good things.*

Joseph has a living monument. It is the Lord's Prayer. *Pray then like this: Our Father.* Now whenever we pray using these words, we are honoring Joseph, who showed our Lord Jesus what a good father on earth is like.

A Social Conscience

CONSCIENCE is a capacity we have which makes us uneasy in wrong-doing. A social conscience means that, when we ourselves are comfortably cared for, we feel uneasy so long as others are in undeserved discomfort.

When we have a social conscience, we refuse to make a separate peace for ourselves in the world war against the giant evils of Disease, Want, Squalor, Ignorance and Unemployment. We refuse to be satisfied with an escape from these evils into a peace and prosperity for ourselves, and to be content to leave God's other children in their cruel clutch.

Some good people have always had a social conscience. Now we need to extend its range and depth, and to make it the guiding and driving power in all social, economic and political life.

A social conscience is a happier companion than personal ambition or private interest.

A social conscience is a more constructive force than the hunger and anger of those who suffer the want and the misery.

Time for Christ's Work

THE first important battle of the Civil War was the battle of Bull Run. General Jackson, by the resolute work of his brigade, won a victory for the Confederates and earned the name of "Stonewall Jackson."

A day or two after the battle, an anxious crowd was gathered at the post office in Lexington, Virginia, General Jackson's home town. They were awaiting news from the front. A letter was handed to Dr. White, Jackson's pastor. He recognized the General's handwriting and hastily opened the letter, exclaiming, "Now we shall learn all the facts!" Here is the letter in full, written the night after the battle:

My dear Pastor:

In my tent last night, after a fatiguing day's service, I remembered that I had failed to send you my contribution to our colored Sunday School. Enclosed you will find my cheque for that object, which please acknowledge at your earliest convenience and oblige yours faithfully,

T. J. JACKSON

General Jackson was one of the great captains of modern times. He was also a Presbyterian elder, interested in Home Missions. He taught in that colored Sunday school in a needy section of his home town. He gave money for it. The night after a great battle he was thinking of the age-long struggle to make his nation a Christian nation, and he began in his home town.

DUTY says, "You must." Love says, "I must." Duty is a kind of coercion; love is Christ constraining. Duty does what is required, and often grudgingly; love does all it can, pouring itself out, with all its treasure, on the unthankful and the evil as well as on the good. Love believes all things, hopes all things. Duty stops at the limit of demands; love goes as far as a Cross.

No moral law could have led Jesus to Calvary, or Livingstone to his lonely death for the black men in Africa.

Duty is like talent, it toils terribly at its task and is proud of its work. Duty does what it can. Love is like genius, it does what it must to fulfill an inner law, the law of Christ. It is moved by a swift creative compulsion, often unaware of its toil. No wonder then that talent is so often vain, and genius so humble. Duty creeps; love has wings.

Duty is fine, but love is the more excellent way. Duty is often harsh and hard; love is gentle and easy to be entreated. Duty is lonely; love is companionable. Duty wearies with its demands; love is refreshed by its responses.

Love is duty redeemed, baptized into the Spirit of Christ. Love is duty doing what Christ asks.

Ennui

BOREDOM by any other name tastes just as cloying.

In these days, when the world is a stage for stupendous events, boredom is the lot of many. Is it because we feel so helpless in the presence of so vast a pageant? We look on it, but do not see our share in it. When we face a crisis, we know it is ours; and we rise to it with dignity. It even thrills us, and we act.

But little things get us down. Hunting lions is great sport; swatting flies is boring. Yet flies are a greater menace to health and life than are lions.

Boredom is sameness, where sameness ought not to be. It is sameness in the mind and spirit. It is sameness where God never meant it to be.

> New every morning is the love
> Our waking and uprising prove.

When we love God, there is no boredom. There is a freshness about every new day. There is adventure in every touch of another life upon ours. People become our hobby. We love our neighbor as ourselves. Exit boredom! Enter the continuing adventure!

Can you read statistics with compassion? When you hear that there are so many millions of people on a starvation diet, can you read these statistics with imagination?

Love and Statistics

Can you see hungry children and the agony of helpless despair in their mothers' faces? Can you look out through the eyes of a father who must watch gaunt death creeping up on his little daughter?

When you see this, and then proceed to do something about it with the same urgency with which you would help a next-door neighbor's hungry child, then you are reading statistics with compassion.

And that is love, a love like Christ's. *When he saw the crowds, he had compassion for them.*

His love was for each one. When He gives us pictures of God's love, He shows love for one lost sheep, for one lost son.

Numbers, however big, are only a repetition of one. One million is just one million times one. And each one is not one millionth of a vast crowd, he is one child of our Father.

49

All
Are
Necessary

THE Arabs have a story of a man who wished to test his sons to find out which of the three loved him best. He sent them out into the world to see which of the three would bring him the most valuable present.

The three brothers met, after a long while, in a distant city, and compared the gifts they had found for their father. The first had a carpet on which he could transport himself and others whithersoever he wished. The second had a medicine which would cure any disease. The third had a glass in which he could see what was going on in any place he desired.

The third used his glass to see what was going on at home. He saw his father ill and in bed. The first transported all three home on his carpet. The second administered his medicine and saved his father's life. The father decided they all loved him equally.

Is labor, capital, or land most useful? Must they all work together for our father?

Now there are varieties of gifts, but the same Spirit; and there are varieties of service, but the same Lord; and there are varieties of working, but it is the same God who inspires them all in every one. (I Corinthians 12:4-6)

Christ in a Hospital

"It is easy to believe in Jesus Christ in a hospital." That is what one patient said to another patient in the men's ward. The other patient exclaimed, "Believe in a hospital? Easy—in a hospital? What do you mean?"

The first patient pointed to a nurse ministering to a sick man near by, and said, "That is the kind of thing Jesus did. He went about doing good. He healed many that were sick. That is what the Bible says. If there had been no Christ, there would have been no hospital. Surely Christ must be in his own house of mercy. It is easy for me to believe in Christ in a hospital."

> Because even here, in this Mansion of Woe,
>   Where creep the dull hours, leaden-shod,
> Compassion and tenderness aid me, I know
>   There is God.

Arthur Guiterman wrote those lines in a hospital.

All the knowledge and skill of physicians and surgeons and nurses are revelations of God, and all their understanding and gentleness are his gifts.

Truly, truly, I say to you, he who believes in me will also do the works that I do. (John 14:12)

Solitude

LONELINESS is thrust upon us. We are left alone. But solitude is something we seek at times if we are wise. Loneliness hurts, solitude heals.

"Our religion is what we do with our solitariness," says a philosopher. Is solitariness a transition between loneliness and solitude, a sort of halfway station? Is it the place where we change trains—trains of thought? We may take the train of loneliness, or of solitude.

If we decide for loneliness, we travel into a cold world of hope laid waste, where thoughts must eat themselves. And cannibal thoughts are no more wholesome companions than cannibal islanders.

If we choose solitude, we turn to the One who is always closer than our heartbeat. We find God in solitude. *Be still, and know that I am God.*

Knowing God is "the bliss of solitude." And knowing God is knowing love, and love is the right way of getting ourselves off our own hands. This is the beginning of health and joy.

> For solitude sometimes is best society,
> And short retirement urges sweet return.

In solitude we can learn to love God and our neighbor—and with those to love, who can be lonely?

The Merciful

THE merciful find many who need their mercy. There is so much which asks our pity: childhood's sorrows, weakness, lonely old age, disease and death. And Christ is the Lord of all who show pity.

Our Lord shows us that pity is the emotion which moves us to do something for pitiable people. He had compassion on the multitudes, and His compassion led Him to the cross that He might destroy sin and death, the things that make life pitiable.

Pity which does nothing is only pernicious hypocrisy, and all the glad surprises at the Judgment Day are for the merciful.

Mercy is the good life touching toil and pain and loss and sin and death. Mercy is not being soft about the sins of others because we don't want to be hard on our own sins. Mercy is helping one who has been hurt by his own sin or another's sin, helping him to believe in the re-creating love of God and, therefore, in a new life with God.

Mercy is not "getting a man off easy"; it is getting him off right. And the merciful find mercy in God and man.

Happiness by the Hard Way

THERE may be no other way. Jesus took the hard way. Seeking to have a humble mind in a proud world, meekness in a world of aggression, the way of mercy in a world of vengeance, a clean heart in a world of pollution, the work of peace in a world of enmity, this can never be an easy way.

The gladness does not come from any and every suffering. It comes from Christ, when we suffer for His sake. We must be sure we are suffering "for righteousness' sake," and not for our self-righteousness. When our suffering is from our self-forgetful loyalty to Him, He is with us in it, and where is deeper joy than with Him?

The hard way is the glad way, because it is the right way. Whence come our most bitter regrets? Do they not come from having tried to make things easy for ourselves? Who ever regrets the silence of meekness, however costly that silence? Who ever wishes unsaid the word of love and peacemaking?

Who ever regrets the long unselfish love to an aging mother? We burn with remorse for the easy ways we took to what we thought would be happiness. The joys we miss are not because of the hardness we endured, but because of the hardness we tried to escape.

The hard way is the way to the Best Society. This road not only leads to the Kingdom of Heaven; we are in the Kingdom all the way—love without self-seeking, purity without self-consciousness, thought without confusion, and work that is not in vain in the Lord.

The Christian life is always possible, but it is never easy.

Accidents

WE bruise our minds over accidents in our Father's world. "Accident" is the Latin word for a "fall." There are many accidents in this, the only world, we yet inhabit. Our Lord was often trying to get us to see our Heavenly Father's care in the best love we find in earthly homes, homes in which the children's falling is somewhere a daily accident.

If we were logical people, we would stop building stairways in houses and chop down all trees in the yards. But stairways and trees seem to be a part of wise building and planting, well worth the risk.

We do not expect stairways to be miraculously removed when the little lad tumbles. And we do not question the love of the father who built the house or kept the tree. A boy, falling down the staircase, does not fall out of his father's care. We pick up little broken sons and heal them in much love.

Do we ask that gravitation be suspended when, as mature men in God's world, we learn to rise above the highest stairway? Do we think that a longer fall can take one of God's children out of His love?

Multiply our best love by the heavenly multiple and see what a sum you get! *How much more will the Heavenly Father! For I am sure that neither ... height, nor depth ... will be able to separate us from the love of God in Christ Jesus our Lord.*

God's gathering up a child of His, whose hurt is past our power to help, is, at least, as gentle and sure as any love we have ever seen on earth.

Encouragement for Mourners

BLESSED *are those who mourn: for they shall be comforted.* If blasted hopes lead to blessedness, then we are all on the way, for he who breathes must suffer; and every thinking man must mourn.

Christians belong to a Kingdom in which the King "learned obedience by the things that He suffered." Christ mourned for sin—not His own, for He had none. But He mourned for our sin and for our griefs. These two forms of mourning are the duty of every believer, and they lead one to blessedness.

Why do we waste energy mourning for the dead who have died in the Lord? They are the guests of God. Save your energy for losses that could be irreparable, like the loss of your true self, the self God means you to be.

Mourn for the life you might have lived. This mourning leads to repentance and the new birth. *If any one is in Christ, he is a new creation.* Mourn for something that God can and will mend.

And in the Kingdom we must mourn for others' pain and loss. The same God who mends broken things cares for them. He who changed you can change them. And when you mourn for others, God shows you how to help Him to help them. "Comforted" does not mean "coddled." It means "strengthened," "fortified."

Calling All Witnesses

ONE Monday I had an errand in the Federal Building. It was a voluntary errand. It took me past the courtrooms. There were anxious-looking people standing in the hall. I asked an officer who they were. He answered that they were witnesses, called under penalty to testify. They knew facts which the court needed to know.

That court represents our organized society; it is our spirit, our mind and will for justice, erected into an institution for the common welfare.

Men are on trial for their lives. A witness may save a man's life. Jesus said, *You shall be my witnesses.*

Do we know anything that can lift up the spirits of men who are in despair? Are we in possession of any facts that can save a man's life?

Christ is the power of God for the saving of every believer. We know His power. *You shall be my witnesses.*

Jesus Christ arose from the dead. Sin and death are defeated. Sin has done his worst and did not win. Death undertook more than he could handle. We know that. *You shall be my witnesses.*

We are not here to argue the case; that is the advocate's job. Our hearsay evidence is not admissible. We are to tell what Christ has done for us.

Anonymous

Kindness

JEAN FREDERIC OBERLIN, who did as much lasting kindness for people as any man of his generation, was once rescued from great danger in the Alps by a peasant. He tried to reward the man for his kindness, but the man refused to take anything.

Oberlin then said, "At least tell me your name so that I may remember you in my prayers."

The peasant replied, "I see you are a preacher. If you will tell me the name of the good Samaritan, then I will tell you my name."

Only God and the innkeeper knew the name of that good man. Certainly Oberlin did not know it. The peasant was aware of that. And this was that humble man's way of saying that the good heart and kind deed are more important than that we should know the name of the person who did it.

We really begin to amount to something to men and to God when we are careful to do kindness and are careless about who gets the credit for it. God knows our names, and He never forgets.

It's
Yours
to Win

Distinguished People

WE WEARY of being mediocre people. We tire of being average members of the masses. Few of us shall ever make the headlines, but we can all become distinguished people. Sainthood is open to us all. We are *called to be saints*. Sainthood is our destiny in Christ.

There is nothing duller than trying to be merely respectable. "Getting-by" morality is as dull as dishwater. There is nothing more exciting than the adventure of letting Christ make distinguished people of us, distinguished for our loving spirit, for our serenity, for our mercy and humility; distinguished for our obedience and faithfulness.

A child was asked, "What is a saint?" He remembered the church windows and answered, "A saint is a person who lets the light shine through." Letting Christ's light shine through us is an exciting adventure.

> Through such souls alone
> God stooping shows sufficient of His light
> For us i' the dark to rise by.

Read I Corinthians 1:1-3.

61

Rooted and Grounded

Have you ever seen a man trying to grow a tuft of edelweiss in his lowland garden? You would never dream that this puny, stricken thing in the garden is a brother to the sturdy plant in the high Alps.

It is an alien here. Its native air is the atmosphere of the heights. The mists of the lower levels hide it from its direct contact with the sun. It cannot bask in the glory of the light. Its name means "noble-white." It cannot be noble-white anywhere but in the radiance of high places.

When, by faith in Christ, our souls are set in their high native air, we also become "noble-white." Moral discernments become clear. No fogs, no murky clouds hide us from Christ's direct light. We live above the low-lying clouds. No longer do we say, "I do not know what is right about this or that." In His light we see light. And we grow like the light to which we are willingly exposed.

Pure affections become a mighty company in us, and we no longer say "We are not interested in this or that work of Christ." We are now *rooted and grounded in love* (Ephesians 3:17), and we come *to the measure of the stature of the fullness of Christ.* (Ephesians 4:13)

We Follow Him

AND because we follow Christ we must not look for an easy way. He never once suggested that we are to have a smooth road. *Then Jesus told his disciples, "If any man would come after me, let him deny himself and take up his cross and follow me."* (Matthew 16:24) *In the world you have tribulation.* (John 16:33) We ought not to be surprised when the going gets rough.

When his daughter Susan complained about some difficulty, Mr. Justice Brandeis said to her, "My dear, if you will just start with the idea that this is a hard world, it would be much simpler." Certainly our Lord told us that this world is not easy for goodness, and His sufferings underscore it with crimson.

Jesus our Lord came not to tell us that the good life is easy; He came to show us that it is possible, and that God is on our side.

It is in prosperity that most people break down. They are not able to manage it. The love of power, the pride of place, the suffocating effects of money and comfort have been the undoing of many. It is the more tragic because they are unaware of their spiritual decay. The sun was our undoing, not the storm. The softest wood in a tree is on the sunny side. It is strong on the side that faces the storm.

We rejoice in our sufferings, knowing that suffering produces endurance, and endurance produces character, and character produces hope. (Romans 5:3-4) *It is enough for the disciple to be like his teacher.* (Matthew 10:25)

63

Very
Present

MUCH of our discussion of problems seems to assume that God is an absentee God. We speak as if He were in the background, working only through moral laws, which He has established, and they carry on for Him while He is away.

The Bible insists that God is present, working now. *God is our refuge and strength, a very present help in trouble. Therefore will not we fear, though the earth be removed.* (Psalm 46:1-2) The Bible is sure that it is not the might of Assyria or the army of Judah with which men must reckon, but with the living, present God.

History is not written in advance, it is written by the fidelity with which we hear and obey the call of God. In every situation there is a challenge from God to us to help Him redeem the situation. He offers us opportunity to share in making history according to His pattern.

General Smuts said, "In the twilight of today I see on the horizon—not the man of Moscow, not the man of Munich, not the man of Rome, but the Man of Galilee."

We Can Know God

WE get more knowledge of God from one square inch of obedience to Him than we get from acres of argument about Him.

How did the scientists discover this now appalling power to split the atom? They obeyed the laws which they already knew. We cannot get religious knowledge without obeying the laws of God which we already know.

Our intellectual assent to truths about Christ brings no saving knowledge of Him; but one decision to dedicate our lives to Him brings new and real knowledge. We may know much theology and yet not know God. We may be experts in grammar and yet not speak good English. We may memorize train schedules but never know the joy of travel.

Our religion is more than correct thinking about God. It is doing His known will for us. Knowledge of God is not something we can work up, as we work up algebra by hard thinking. The knowledge of God comes by hard choosing at the place where we meet the will of God for us, and say "yes."

Jesus said, *If any man's will is to do his will, he shall know whether the teaching is from God.* (John 7:17)

Reading the Gospels

When Jesus Christ seems unreal and far away, separated from us by dim tracts of time, try reading a Gospel autobiographically. Read on steadily until you come to the story of someone who came to Jesus with a great need like your own present need.

Let us suppose that your burden is a child, your own child, or the child of a friend. The child's personality is warped; he is a misery to himself and to those who love him. Read until you come to Matthew 17:14-18. A father brings his son to Christ. Now read it autobiographically. It is your story. You are responsible for a child who is throwing himself into the fires of dissipation. Read it, *A man came up to him and kneeling before him said, "Lord, have mercy on my son."*

Then see the dividing mists of time scatter; and see Christ standing before you. He has the same love for you that He had for the man in the Gospel story. He is as truly available to you and to your child as He was then. He is saying now to you, *Bring him here to me.*

Find the situation that is like yours, and then walk right into that picture with Christ, who is *the same yesterday and today and forever.*

I Have Seen

In years now past I used to go often to the Swiss Alps to a village in the Bernese Oberland, called Lauterbrunnen. Alp on alp rises above it. Often for days on end we saw no mountains, nothing but the slopes above the valley and rocks lost in the mists. Then a morning came and we saw the miracle of the mountain peaks. We bathed our spirits in the glory of the sight. Then the clouds came down again blotting out everything.

Some people came, stayed a day or two, and went away having seen nothing of the majesty of the peaks. But we had seen, we knew. Nothing could make us doubt the glory that was there.

Looking to Jesus; we have seen Him. He is there, though mists of doubt come down and hide Him from us for days on end, still He is there, alive forevermore.

Wait patiently for him. Though the vision tarry, wait for it, because it will surely come. You saw Him once, you shall see Him again. The mists may obscure Him for a little while, but they cannot take Him away from His place with us. "His foundation is in the holy mountains."

The Habit of Hope

WE are never really defeated except when we have a traitor within our own gates. There is one near to us, so near that if it is not the Devil it is a very despicable self; he keeps whispering comments on all you have done or plan: "I don't think you can win. The enemy is very strong. Better look for some easy way out. You failed yesterday! Remember last week! last year!" And if we listen long to him we are beaten before we begin.

The citadel of the soul is never taken except when a betrayer from within opens the gates. He wins our consent to his traitorous work by destroying hope in us. He makes us think of our own scant resources, of our rusty sword, our paper armor and our feeble right arm.

It is the work of the Spirit of God to remind us that we are soldiers under authority of the King. The Spirit bids us look to Him. He is mighty. His sword is sharp. His armor is shining and strong. He is able. "Christ executeth the office of a king, in subduing us to himself, in ruling and defending us, and in restraining and conquering all his and our enemies." The old Westminster Divines wrote that into the Shorter Catechism. I would far rather have written that sentence than Gray's "Elegy."

Learn the habit of hope. *I am sure that he who began a good work in you will bring it to completion.*

Cast the traitor out. In 1631 a ship sailed from England to explore dangerous and unknown regions. One of the articles to which the crew swore allegiance was that "no man shall speak a despairing word against the success of the expedition, or make a doubt thereof."

It's Yours to Conquer It

Some foreigners come to our shores as to a promised land. The shadow of old-world oppression is still upon them. They set forth, with beautiful poignancy, their visions of what they expect to find here.

They look for liberty already won, a freedom provided like a "ready-to-wear" suit of clothes. They expect to have it given to them; and they come to receive it, not to achieve it. They come with the feeling that when they arrive in New York the struggle is over. And they are disappointed. For none of God's best gifts can be "grabbed up."

"The Promised Land" of the Israelites was not given over to them unincumbered, clear and ready for their comfortable occupancy. It was full of enemies. There were *Amorites, Hittites, Perizzites, Hivites, and Jebusites, which were not of the children of Israel.* They had to wrest it from the enemies of "the good life." There was a warfare to be waged; battles must be fought. They had to subdue and earn it before they could have and hold.

We never receive any *land which he promised* conquered, cleared, ready for the occupancy of our lazy souls. If we did, we would be too feeble to keep it. "The Promised Land" is ours—the good life is ours—to be won. None but the conqueror can receive.

Do you want to discover the joy of nearness to God? Do you want to feel His power possessing your soul? Then undertake something for Him which is too great and beautiful for you to accomplish without coming back again, and yet again, to Him. Do that, and abide in His presence.

Friends Are Free

FREE is from an old English verb *freon*, to love. The only survivor from that family is *friend*. There is Providence in that fact. Only friends are free. There is no freedom except in friendship.

Friends do not kill one another when they are vexed. There is a restraint of love, and the restraint is the basis of freedom. Every *Thou shalt not* yields a great freedom. We are free only in a society where friends lay restraints upon themselves.

Liberty, in the sense of "doing what you please," is something the foolish cry for; liberty, in the sense of personal responsibility, is the very thing most people do not want.

Democracy is a stern and lofty creed of willing self-denial and of responsibility stanchly born, or it degenerates into a stampede for power and gain. "The man who spiritualizes democracy will save the world," said Mazzini.

Jesus said, *You are my friends*. Friends make one another free. Christ alone can spiritualize democracy. Christ makes men friends across all frontiers and over all barriers.

WE complain often about our failures of memory. This is a matter of regret; but is inability to remember, or inability to forget, your bitterest problem?

Teach Me to Forget

"Teach me to forget," said Themistocles bitterly to one who offered to improve his memory.

Our memories work overtime, and ask no extra pay for it, in recalling hurts and slights and scornful remarks. How much of our waking thoughts are of things it would be our joy to be able to forget? Our problem is quite as much a problem of how to forget as it is how to remember.

William James says that one great function of our minds is forgetting. We need to thank God that He has made us so we can forget some things. And the art of happy living is bound up with suitable forgetting.

Forgetting what lies behind and straining forward to what lies ahead, I press on toward the goal for the prize of the upward call of God in Christ Jesus. (Philippians 3:13-14) Believe in God; accept His future for you; go to work for it. Give your thoughts a new center of association. Christ is this new center. You can forget by remembering Christ.

A
Door

A SCOTTISH-BORN friend tells an event from the village of his boyhood. A man bought a handsome door from a demolished house. It was a door of superior lineage; it had once had a fine setting; it was beautiful; and it came to him almost as free as God's grace.

He built the fine door into the wall of his old house, a house unlike its original setting. The effect offended his eyes. The door made the wall look mean and low.

Then he decided he needed a new house; and he built a new house to fit the fine door. His mind had peace. "All things were now done decently and in order."

Jesus said, *I am the door.* Certain it is that if we take this Door, we shall have a new house to fit the Door—new walls, new windows, a new and hospitable hearth, a new Spirit dwelling in the innermost. *If any one is in Christ, he is a new creation.*

> With all my being rearranged,
> Pass'd through the crucible of time.

He Believed God

"He believed God and did his duty." That is the inscription cut into a simple stone such as marked the grave of every soldier. They are the words on the grave of General Haig in Dryburgh Abbey.

In the *Life of Haig* is this story: "On the darkest day of all—Sunday, March 24, 1918—he appeared as usual at the church service on the ramparts of Montreuil. Duncan, the minister, taking a risk few of those who worked with Haig would have ventured to take, said as the chief shook hands with him before the service, 'I hope things are not too bad, sir.' Haig replied, 'They will never be too bad. This is what you read to us a few weeks ago in church: *Be not afraid, nor dismayed by reason of this great multitude; for the battle is not yours, but God's.*'" (II Chronicles 20:15)

That evening Haig faced the great crisis of the First World War, and he did not fail. "He believed God and did his duty." He was a good soldier of Jesus Christ.

Believing God and doing our duty is a path which is open to each one of us.

May

I
Present?

WE HAVE pleasure in introducing people whom we love. Peter tells us that Christ suffered in order that He might introduce us to God as His friends. *For Christ also died for sins once for all, the righteous for the unrighteous, that he might bring us to God.* (I Peter 3:18) *Bring* really means *introduce.* Christ suffered for the right to bring us to God, and to say, "Father, these are my friends."

There was a barrier of guilt in our hearts. We had sinned; and we did not want to meet God. We were resentful, blaming God for our losses. Christ loves us into repentance; He wins us to a changed heart by His suffering for our sins.

Then He takes us by the hand, and presents us to His Father and our Father and says, "Father, these are my friends. They care for people, not for power; they help one another; they no longer use one another. They endure suffering; they no longer cause suffering. They bear one another's burdens, and so fulfill my law. They belong to our family now; they belong with us."

"Adoption is an act of God's free grace, whereby we are received into the number, and have a right to all the privileges, of the sons of God." (The Shorter Catechism)

The Way of Escape

WE HAVE God's assurance that there is *the way of escape.* Here it is: *No temptation has overtaken you that is not common to man. God is faithful, and he will not let you be tempted beyond your strength, but with the temptation will also provide the way of escape, that you may be able to endure it.* (I Corinthians 10:13)

We are to escape not by dodging the temptation but by meeting it; not by going around it, but by going right through it with our trust in God triumphant. Suppose a man is in a position of trust; and he is tempted to take money that belongs to others. He could dodge the temptation by resigning his position. That is an escape, but not the one God promises. God promises power to make him trustworthy in the job. This is the only way of escape that the Bible recognizes as good.

The temptation now *common to man* is despair; and there is no way round it. There is a way up through it. The word here translated *the way of escape* means "a going up out." The way up to God remains and will remain open to all of us. No one but ourselves can drop an iron curtain between us and God. He will give us power to bear what must be borne. *Ask, and it will be given you.* (Matthew 7:7)

Our Tools

WHEN a man entered the order founded by Francis of Assisi, if he possessed any property, he gave that away, but he kept the tools of his trade.

In Christ's service we are still businessmen or physicians; we are scholars or laborers; we are young or old; strong in body or frail; we are men or women; we have white skins or black.

We keep the tools of race and of body and all the skills of our brains and hands. But now they are in the service of our Lord Christ. We use them willingly for Him and under His direction.

What matters is not the number of our tools, whether one or five or two, but that we bring them all with us into His service.

It does not take much of a man to be a Christian, but it does take all there is of him.

Read Matthew 25:14-30.

Victory

over

Time

NANSEN tells us in *Farthest North* how he reached the North Pole. He discovered, by his explorations in the polar seas, that there is a steady drift of ice across the uncharted regions of the Pole. He decided that this drift would carry a ship over the place of the North Pole. The problem, therefore, was to join the drift. He built his ship, the *Fram*. It was constructed strong enough to stand the pressure of the ice. He put her into the pack ice north of Siberia. She was frozen in and, after three years, came out north of Spitzbergen. The drift had carried her right over the polar regions. Which thing is a parable.

There are many currents in our world. We did not create them. They are strong; we cannot control them. If we are once caught up into one of them, we are carried by it in spite of ourselves.

But we have power to choose the "drift" into whose stream we surrender the movement of our life. This is under the sovereign control of our own wills.

Our chief business is to be reminded of the "drift" toward God. We had no power to set that happy movement agoing. God began that in Christ. It is a majestic drift. It moves across the seas of the centuries, catching up the many who have been willing to join its saving current, and carries them to their desired haven, the harbor of God's love.

You will join some drift. You have joined already, because you *must*. It is the way life has with us. Have you joined the right drift? There is a stout ship (she has weathered many storms) going into the drift toward God.

79

Optimism

or

Hope

Optimism and hope are not the same. They are two things, and different.

Optimism is a temperament; it is the result of steady nerves and a good digestion. Hope is an achievement of the soul, and it is a force. Optimism is a view, a rosy view, of life which we may hold in advance of experience. Hope is born out of the experience of life itself, out of trouble and sorrow and faith and enduring love.

Optimism is built upon theory and circumstantial arrangements. Hope is personal conviction growing out of the discernment that within the world order there is harmony and the purpose of God.

In optimism we vaguely expect that something good will turn up. In hope we are convinced by our experience that there is such a thing as eternity, and that time is a part of it, and that God is the King over it all.

For I know the thoughts that I think toward you, saith the Lord, thoughts of peace, and not of evil. (Jeremiah 29:11)

And So On

How far does life go? Is our life only in time? Or does our life find its significance in something beyond time? We belong to the generation of the uncertain.

We live with people who have thrown away eternity so that they may be free to kill time. They have doomed themselves to a journey without compass or road maps— to a journey in a desert which has boundaries but no horizon. They see no future because they have no faith.

But we have a future, because we belong to God; and time and eternity are His. We have no time to kill, because our time belongs to our eternal life in God.

We know why we are here. The Everlasting Father put us here for His purposes of love. We have horizons, and they blend with the infinite.

We have compass and road maps, in the life and teachings of our Lord Jesus Christ. We have a way right through death, in the resurrection of Him, who is the way, the truth and the life. So we go right on.

Climate and Destiny

"Of all strong things, none is more wonderfully strong than man. . . . Language is his, and wind-swift thought, and city-founding mind; and he has learned to shelter himself from cold and piercing rain." So wrote Sophocles.

The fault is not in our climate but in ourselves if we are underlings. We are master of waters and airs and places. Humidities, worse than rain, soak and drench us, but we have air-conditioning.

We count it no shame and take shelter from the weather. That is our wisdom, and we do it that we may conserve strength and gather energy to work. The wise soldier thinks it no weakness to take cover that he may live to fight another day.

God is our refuge from the stormy blast, and our eternal home.

Why let yourself be frightened by such words as "escape mechanism"? Take refuge in God from the weather which you have created by wrong act and habit; find shelter in his grace, and new energy; and keep a base of operations in the mercy of God.

The climate of Christ's presence is your destiny. He creates the right climate; it is yours to choose it, and the choice is destiny.

The Hand of God

In the Academy at Florence there stand several blocks of marble. Those blocks of marble have the marks of Michael Angelo's chisel on them. You can see the dim outlines of massive figures beginning to emerge from the marble. But they are still imprisoned in it; they are still in the rough. They are called "The Prisoners."

The artist intended to make them part of the magnificent tomb of Julius II. It was never completed; so "The Prisoners" are still imprisoned. They seem to be waiting for the touch of the hand that can set them free. But now they can never be released; Michael Angelo is dead.

We are Christians in the making; we are still in the rough. There is so much yet to be done for us by the Great Artist's hand. And we have hope without limit, because the Creative Hand at work on us is the Hand of our Living Lord.

The world is waiting for the revealing of the Sons of God in us. (Romans 8:19) Christ is alive; His touch has still its ancient power. We are confident that He who began a good work in us will perfect it.

We are not meant to adorn a tomb; He plans to make us fellow citizens with the saints in the City of the Living God.

Is It
Quantity?

MERE quantity has little meaning when it is applied to human life. The man in the Bible who got the greatest quantity has a short and pathetic biography: *And all the days of Methuselah were nine hundred sixty and nine years: and he died.* He was long on quantity; he was short on quality.

Is this God's way of suggesting that mere quantity is not enough?

Our Lord Jesus Christ lived a scant three decades, and the record covers not much more than two years. Nine hundred sixty-nine is to thirty-three—how much? Well, it is very little.

There is a quality in Christ's short years that has led us to make all our calendars begin with His birth. There was a quality in His few years that has made all our lives significant.

He has moved more men upward than any other person who has ever walked this planet.

Methuselah missed the quality in the midst of quantity. The quality may be found in one moment with Christ. God gives eternal life for enjoying the quality.

Quantity without quality is what discerning souls call hell.

The Best Way to Explain

"THE best way to explain it is to do it," said the Dodo in *Alice in Wonderland*. That is good theology and the best religion.

The best way to explain the existence of God is to do what He asks. The best way to explain love is to be loving. The best way to explain forgiveness is to be forgiving. The best way to explain eternal life is to live it.

Isn't this Jesus' way of explaining the greatest truths? He did not prove the existence of God by logic; He showed us by living the life of a child of the Father. He did not argue about the possibility of immortality; He lived the kind of life that is worth continuing, the kind of life that would make us glad to be immortal.

We are not here to argue for God; we are here to live for Him. Any smart person can show up the flaws in our logic, but who can gainsay our glad and obedient life with Christ?

The best way to explain your faith in Christ is just to live it.

Saved
by
Serving

Unamuno, the Spanish philosopher, tells about the Roman aqueduct at Segovia, in his native Spain. It was built in the year of our Lord 109. For eighteen hundred years it carried cool water from the mountains to the hot and thirsty city. Nearly sixty generations of men drank from its flow.

Then came another generation, a recent one, who said, "This aqueduct is so great a marvel that it ought to be preserved for our children's children, as a kind of museum piece. We shall relieve it of its centuries-long labor." They did; they laid modern iron pipes.

They gave the ancient bricks and mortar a reverent rest. And the aqueduct began to fall apart. The sun beating on the dry mortar caused it to crumble. The bricks and stones sagged and threatened to fall. What ages of service could not destroy idleness disintegrated.

We are saved by serving. No work which God lays upon us will do other than make us strong. Our task from God is our life preserver.

Victory over Time

WE HAVE had many notable victories over space. A motorcar is a victory over space; so also is a streamliner train, and an airplane, and a radio. But time still beats us back and defeats us.

Twenty-four hours are still required to turn the earth on its axis. Three hundred and sixty-five days, and no less, roll the earth around the sun. We have no machinery which will stretch a day or compress it.

Memory and printing are partial victories over time; they save some riches out of time's ruins. But the only real victory over time is in Christ. We triumph over time whenever we make a day or an hour yield such a quality of life as is *fit* to last forever.

We triumph over time when we use time to create a relationship with Christ that shall outlast time. In the moment when we respond to the love of the Eternal Father, in that moment we have eternal life; and this is the victory over time.

And this is eternal life, that they know thee the only true God, and Jesus Christ whom thou hast sent. (John 17:3)

Statuesque Christians

I RECALL the thrill of my first sight of Verrocchio's statue of Colleoni in Little Saint Mark's Square in Venice.

A masterful man sits astride a powerful horse. The power of the horse is the plaything of the rider's will. His feet are firmly in the stirrups. The baton of command is in his hand. It is the picture of masterfulness. The horse is so much a living thing that you look to see him bound off the pedestal.

Many times I have gone back since that first visit to Venice just to see the man on the horse, commanding such power. But as often as I have gone back to see him, he is exactly in the same place.

He makes one think of some Christians. They seem to have everything. They have command of great power. They have all the appearance of masterfulness. They seem always to be on the point of doing great things. But as often as you see them through the years they are in the same place.

It is pose not poise, potential not performance. They are only statuesque Christians. They need to come alive in Christ.

Lost and Found

OUR Lord Jesus often used the word *lost* where we use *sinner*. He uses *sin* and *sinner* very sparingly. He preferred the word *lost*. Did he use *lost* because *sinner* describes our feelings about ourselves? It emphasizes what we have done to ourselves, and it tends to leave us shut in with our own shame and failure.

Lost tells us that we are lost to Someone. It expresses God's feelings about us: we are out of our place at His side and in danger of not getting back to Him.

All the lost things, and all the lost sons, are lost to someone. Someone has lost us. We are lost to our real selves. The coin fell out of the woman's purse and rolled away. The sheep wandered away from the shepherd. The prodigal son deliberately packed up and left his father. We are lost to God our Father. His heart is grieved over the loss.

We do not have to remain lost. We do not even have to find the way home for ourselves. Someone is seeking us. The woman with her broom is seeking her coin. The shepherd is seeking his sheep. The father's love goes out in search of his son, and on the beam of his father's love he comes home.

Our Father is seeking us, and He will seek until He finds us. Read Luke, Chapter 15.

Prisoners of Hope

WE ARE all prisoners, prisoners of our desires, of our work, of our imperious duties, of our longings, but all prisoners. We shall never escape from prison, but we can choose our prison.

So many are prisoners of the unimportant. They cannot see the stars because they are so busy playing at tiddly-winks. They fritter away their destiny because they have no vision. They are not prodigals, squandering their substance on riotous living. They are only jailed by the unimportant.

Turn you to the strong hold, ye prisoners of hope. (Zechariah 9:12) We are still prisoners. But hope is the walls, and hope is the bars, and hope our jailer and our prison food. Hope is the sure expectation of good from our God in the world He has made. *For thou art my hope, O Lord God.* (Psalm 75:5)

May the God of hope fill you with all joy and peace in believing, so that by the power of the Holy Spirit you may abound in hope. (Romans 15:13)

The Beatitudes

Happy is the meaning of the Greek word we translate *blessed*. The word *happy* seems to come closer to us. The Sermon on the Mount begins: *Happy are . . .*

We have an instinct for happiness. We never doubt our capacity for joy. The verdict of humanity on life is that we are created for happiness. Jesus begins the Constitution of His Kingdom with *happy*.

He does not question our right to happiness. He does question the ways we take to find it. He sees us taking our infinite needs to earth's poor storehouses; offering our hungry souls provender from larger barns. We thought happiness was in having this and that. He tells us that it is being His kind of person.

The Beatitudes are nothing less than our Lord's description of Himself. These are the qualities that make His life the blessed life. This is the kind of life we would ask to have continued to all eternity. He came that we may have this life and have it more abundantly. Read Matthew 5:1-16.

Called To Be Saints

A SAINT is just a sinner in the re
making, a soul being emancipated
from the love of self and in process
of being enslaved by the love of
Christ. The saint is just a man who has chosen between the
two masters.

This choice has a definite beginning. At some clear place
of decision we choose Christ instead of ourselves. And the
choice must be made again and yet again, for the perseverance of the saints is a continual stream of new beginnings.

The first of Luther's ninety-five theses is that the Christian life is a daily repentance and conversion—a turning to
Christ every day.

A saint then, as everywhere in the New Testament, is
just a person who is committed to Christ. He knows what
he wants in this world, and realizes joyfully how much he
can do without. He knows what he wants to do and what
he wants to have, and he knows that he will be joyful when
all else vanishes and leaves him at his chosen job of being
a fellow-worker together with Christ.

The saint is the man of Christ's *Blesseds*. And the only
final sorrow is not to be one.

Living

by the

Day

ABOUT the time Columbus was looking for a New World a Chinese
philosopher gave a sound suggestion
for improving an old one. His name
was Wang, and his prescription is this:

"The ancients, who wished to promote illustrious virtue
throughout the Empire, first put their own states in good
order.

"Wishing to put their own states in order, they first regu-
lated their own families.

"Wishing to regulate their own families, they first set
themselves right.

"Wishing to set themselves right, they purified their own
hearts.

"Wishing to purify their own hearts, they first sought to
be sincere in their thoughts."

That brings us down out of generalities. The world will
not be better until we are better people. We shall never have
a better century until the hours and days are better. In fact
the better century begins with your next seconds.

Wang of China and White of Emporia agree. "This
world is made better by every man improving his own con-
duct—no reform is accomplished wholesale."

Conversion is the real reformation. *Unless you turn and
become like children, you will never enter the kingdom of
heaven.* (Matthew 18:3)

A
Miracle
for Marriage

OUR Lord's first miracle was for marriage. He healed the sick, he gave sight to the blind, he raised the dead, he fed the hungry, but he began his mighty works for a husband and wife.

There were vast and complicated problems of government, and industry and education, and social welfare, problems such as confront us today. But Jesus began with a home and a marriage.

There was a marriage at Cana in Galilee. . . . Jesus also was invited to the marriage with his disciples. (John 2:1-2) And he brought them a miracle. They must not be shamed before their guests. He saved them from shame.

This, the first of his signs Jesus did at Cana in Galilee, and manifested his glory. (John 2:11) And he continues his miracles for marriage in every home to which he is bidden.

The first wine of married joys may fail, but Christ has a better wine, the joy of united obedience. He said, *Where two or three are gathered in my name, there am I in the midst.* A husband and a wife make two, and they are enough. And where there is a child you have the three.

New homes, and homes made new, could make a new world for us by this evening.

Bible Translators

A young Durham miner invited one of his friends to go with him to a meeting of the Bible Society which which was to be held in their neighborhood.

His friend asked, "What have you to do with the Bible Society?"

The young miner answered, "I'm a translator."

The friend exclaimed, "What! You a translator? What language do you know?"

The miner replied, "I know the English Bible, and the language of daily life, and I am busy every day translating the New Testament into my daily life."

That is the truly modern translation—better than "Moffat" or "Weymouth," or any "Revised Version." This is the "Revived Version," the version that is lived again—the version of the Bible in your life.

The Bible was in life before it was written, and we translate it back into life. Any translator's life is full of hard, exacting work. But it opens God's Word to many of His children. And our version is the first that many read.

Read II Corinthians 3:1-3.

Don't
Worry

PROFESSOR NORBERT WIENER at M.I.T. holds that there is much in common between our brain and a machine.

He believes that the brain has its limitations, like a telephone system which has barely enough switchboards for the normal calls of its customers. It has ample capacity for our real needs, but it works close to capacity.

We may call the grocer and the doctor; make business arrangements; ring up our friends to offer help—in short, do all our regular dialing—and the machine is able to handle it.

But if all over town jittery Jimmies and anxious Annies begin to make needless calls for police, false alarms to the fire department, silly calls about trash collecting and a thousand more about phantom fears, then the system already working near capacity breaks down.

So in our brain malignant worry, by taking over too many connections for its continual circulations of patterns of anxious thoughts, does not leave the worried person sufficient nerve energy for his normal needs for living.

Jesus said, *Do not be anxious.* Trust and hope and love and peace keep our minds free for their proper functions.

Living by the Day

LIVING by the day is the only way we can live. We are all day laborers; we do our work by the day or not at all. We work by the day even when we are paid by the month. In truth we work by the hour, and we live by the hour. We are day laborers and day livers, hour workers and hour livers.

Trouble comes when we try to live yesterday over again, and when we try to live tomorrow before it comes. That spells worry. Jesus gave all harassed and tired people some homely advice: *Therefore do not be anxious about tomorrow, for tomorrow will be anxious for itself. Let the day's own trouble be sufficient for the day.* (Matthew 6:34)

He is saying, "If you must worry, then worry about one day at a time; not about yesterday, for it is now in God's hands; not about tomorrow, for God has not yet given it to us. The only way to make a life of care and work tolerable is to take it in daily installments." That would reduce our worry by two thirds, and even that is desirable.

Keep your worries all for today, because it is for today that God gives us bread; it is for today that God promises strength. *As thy days, so shall thy strength be.* (Deuteronomy 33:25) And he asks us to carry our cross only a day at a time. *If any man will come after me, let him . . . take up his cross daily.* (Luke 9:23)

Traveling with Ourselves

SOCRATES was once asked, "Why is it that Alcibiades, who is so brilliant, and has traveled so widely, and has seen so much of the world, is still such an unhappy man?"

Socrates answered, "Because wherever he goes Alcibiades takes himself with him."

Could this explain why southern California has so many queer and restless people? It is easy, if we have a funded income, to retire from a farm or from a business. Those can be left where they are; but it is not so easy to retire from an anxious, unhappy self.

Getting away from the difficulties of our family life does not suddenly make us contented people.

Wherever we go we take ourselves with us, and we are not good traveling companions until we are good people.

This is why Jesus offers to be our companion. We cannot live with Him and not be better people. When we live with Him we always have good company, and we are good company.

The Filling Station

HAVE you ever seen God at a filling station? Not God at filling stations, when you stop to replenish your failing source of power!

Did God never speak to you at a filling station? Did you never hear Him saying to you, "Why so careful about this kind of power, and why so careless about My kind of power?"

Has God never yet made your act of filling the tank sacramental? Do you never think as the gauge runs up, "Certainly I need Christ's power; and I will stop at His power stations. I will pull up, on my journey, for prayer and worship and Bible reading. I need to look at that Road Map. My vision is not so clear as it ought to be. I can use some help on cleaning my windshield, that the eyes of my heart may be enlightened. I need at least a little of the 'oil of joy.'"

Read Ephesians 3:14-19.

Another
Freedom

WE NEED another freedom—emancipation from the past. Between rankling regrets for yesterday and anxious doubts about tomorrow many Christians spend their whole lives. This leaves no time, no energy for rejoicing in God our Saviour right now.

It is worse than futile to hunt yesterday's rabbit over again, especially the one that got away. Our brain cells are our capital, and we can squander them foolishly, in a way that yields no dividends.

Hunting yesterday's rabbit is the specialty of many sensitive souls with high ideals. Surely we have lessons to learn from the past. Learn them quickly in the presence of the Lord, leaving Him to deal with what has gone beyond our control. "He robs himself that spends a bootless grief."

Leave the past with God; use the present for work with Him, and He will lead us into the future.

The long-distance runner wastes little time on frequent glances over his shoulder. The man in the hundred-yard dash wastes none. He looks forward.

Let us also lay aside every weight, and sin which clings so closely, and let us run with perseverance the race that is set before us, looking to Jesus the pioneer and perfecter of our faith, who for the joy that was set before him endured the cross. (Hebrews 12:1-2)

The Luxury of Choice

Men liberated from enemy prison camps know the blessed luxury of choice. They may choose their food, where they will walk, and their companions.

But what of those of us who are ill? What of those who are shut in with sorrow? What of those whose years add up to loneliness and failing strength for the work they love? Have we any blessed luxury of choice?

We have. We can still choose the spirit in which we meet these changes. We can still choose how we shall carry our sorrow, and how we shall deal with our loneliness. We cannot always choose our burdens, but we can always choose how we shall bear them.

And this choice is just as real as the choice of a road, or a coat, or a car.

Our Saviour was compelled to go to the cross. He chose the kind of spirit which He took to the cross.

Our sufferings do color the very texture of our souls. But we can choose the color.

Work . . .
Today

THIS is God's command to us. Our work for our Father must all be done within the confines of a "today." Tomorrow is the day when the lazy work. Tomorrow is the day when the foolish plan to repent. Tomorrow is the Devil's today.

A man had two sons; and he went to the first and said, "Son, go and work in the vineyard today." (Matthew 21:28)

My Father asks me to work today. Today I must plant and water vines that in some other day will bear rich fruit. Today I must be patient; I must not complain because planting and harvest are not in the same today.

I must not forget that the fruits of the spirit are not gathered in the day of planting. Today I must do His will, and God, who made seedtime and harvest, will appoint a today for gathering the increase.

Today all my activities must be His appointments; all my errands His errands. Today my Father says, *Son, go and work . . . today.*

Do It for God

Our work can be very monotonous. It can also be very exhilarating. The difference between monotony and exhilaration is mostly in us.

An old Negro working in the engine room of a Great Lakes steamer was heard singing:

> Oh, you gotta get a glory
> In the work you do;
> A Hallelujah Chorus
> In the heart of you.
>
> Paint, or tell a story,
> Sing, or shovel coal;
> But you gotta get a glory
> Or the job lacks soul.

The old Negro found a way to make coal shoveling a glorious work. The glory of God in the Bible means the revelation of God's character. The simplehearted old man found that God could be revealed in the way coal was handled.

We have to get a glory in the work we do.

It has been computed that the average married woman will have to wash three hundred and forty tons of dirty dishes in her lifetime—three million dishes. She needs to get a glory in the work she does. The average man will work one hundred thousand hours before he retires on his pension. This counts up to six million minutes. A little glory in *each* of those minutes adds up to a radiant life.

And whatever you do, in the word or deed, do everything in the name of the Lord Jesus, giving thanks to God the Father through him. (Colossians 3:17) This is the way to get a glory in the work we do.

105

The Lighted Mind

THE condition of sight is a moral condition. Vision is determined by character. The things we miss seeing are the things we miss being. Every wrong done dims the inward eye; every true deed is a revelation of God. The impure see everything but God.

To see God in the day's work requires a pure heart. To see God in the face of an innocent child requires a pure heart. To see God in the love of a good woman requires a pure heart. To see God in the suffering and the judgment upon our time needs a better lens than the cloudy and crooked spectacles of cynicism.

Our view depends on our point of view. There is a cellar view and a mountain view. We see more from the clean heights of pure thoughts.

But cleaning up the heart is Christ's work. We cannot remove the soil and stain. God be thanked! There is the new birth. We can, and must, be born again. He who created can re-create.

Are you weary of an impure heart? Then *ask, and it will be given you.*

A SCHOLAR in a mission Sunday-school class in Africa was asked, "What would you have said if you had been the king, when the daughter of Herodias asked for the head of John the Baptist on a platter?" The scholar said, "I would have answered, 'John the Baptist's head belongs to the half of the kingdom I did not promise.'"

When Abraham Lincoln was asked to do a thing of doubtful honesty, it was urged on him, "Nobody will know it." Lincoln replied, "Yes, they will. Abraham Lincoln will know it, and I have to sleep with him."

A Negro lad stood in the slave market waiting to be sold to a new owner. A man whom the boy knew to be kind to his slaves said to him, "If I buy you, will you be honest?" The Negro slave boy replied, "I'll be honest whether you buy me or not."

Socrates, the greatest of the Greek Thinkers, is famous for asking the right questions. We Christians can be famous for giving the right answers.

But in your hearts reverence Christ as Lord. Always be prepared to make a defense to any one who calls you to account for the hope that is in you, yet do it with gentleness and reverence; and keep your conscience clear. (I Peter 3:15-16)

The Great Venture

FAITH is the great venture. It is acting on the truth we have. It is putting truth to the test of living it. It is not leaning back and saying, "O yes, I accept that truth"; it is living by that truth. We all live every day by faith, else no one would cross a bridge, take a train, marry a wife, or learn a new truth.

Faith is what we do about the truth we see. Jesus never once attempted to give us a definition of faith. He saw God as Father, and proceeded to live His life on that basis. On the cross He said, *Father, into thy hands I commit my spirit!* And God raised Him from the dead. His faith in God was proved true by His life.

How can we know that God is good? We cannot be sure, not absolutely sure in advance. We can only take Christ's Word for it, and the word of other Christians who have put His Word to the test and found Him true. Then we put His Word to the test for ourselves.

> Are there not, dear Michal,
> Two points in the adventure of the diver,
> One—when, a beggar, he prepares to plunge,
> One—when, a prince, he rises with his pearl?
> Festus, I plunge!

We live by faith, and God responds to our faith. *Therefore God is not ashamed to be called their God, for he has prepared for them a city.* (Hebrews 11:16)

Good Manners

GOOD manners are so much a part of our life that Jesus preached sermons on manners for Christians. *Manners* comes from a Latin word *manus* which means hand. Our manners are the way we handle our relationships with people.

There are good ways of handling them, and there are bad ways. It is like tact; tact is our touch on other lives. I wonder why tact is always good or it is not tact. We never speak of good tact and bad tact.

The essence of good manners is our sense of the value of other people. We handle valuable things reverently. Every person is worth the cost of the cross of Christ. We must treat him respectfully. And the height of rudeness is acting as though a man does not count. One human soul equals the cross of Christ; this is the Gospel equation. This gives Jesus His amazing courtesy.

And this right sense of the value of people to God gives us a sense of leisure. God took time to create them; He had patience with them; He listens to their prayers. Surely they are worth a little of our time. The rude man is usually a little man in a hurry about little things.

Jesus always had time for people, because people count with Him. And a conversation with Him was a dialogue, not a monologue. *What do you think?* He would ask, and He waited for the answer.

Read Luke 14:7-14 and Romans 14:15.

Evening and Morning

AND *the evening and the morning were the first day.* So the Book says. (Genesis 1:5)

We would say, "There was morning and there was evening one day." But is not the Book right?

The evening determines the day. It is the evening that brings the morning after. We awake in the mood that held us when we fell asleep. *Do not let the sun go down on your anger.* And why not? Because the sun that sets on your anger will rise on it again?

God set the bounds of the day that there may be an end of the day's irritations. We dare not carry today's evil across the divide of sleep. We must be done with it.

By some definite act of humility and of love before God, by some pledge of amendment and reparation, ask God, for Christ's sake, to forgive, to take away today's evil mood.

Learning

to

Pray

Prizing Our Silences

Do WE overestimate the worth of our speaking and of our doing? The Old Testament suggests that we stand still and see the salvation that God works for us. We are told to wait upon the Lord, to be still and know that God is. Do we prize silence enough?

Our Lord prized His silences. Early in the morning, a great while before day, He went out alone into a mountain to pray. He went into silence in his Temptation. There He found God's best way to help us. At the Transfiguration He overheard Moses and Elijah speaking of the Exodus which He was to accomplish for all the enslaved children of God. In Gethsemane He left even His most understanding friends, and went farther to be alone with God, to find His will and to accept it.

All of His deepest experiences are set in a zone of silence. He asked from His friends nothing but that they watch with Him before God.

Prayer is not so much our going to God with beseeching words, as it is God's coming to us with His delivering Word. This requires from us humble, waiting minds. *Speak, Lord; for thy servant heareth.* We prize our silences, because in them we hear His voice.

How We Get More Faith

"IF ONLY I had more faith!" How often we say that. If we had more faith, God would be real to us; we would have courage for dark days and light on our perplexities. If we had more faith, we could turn our city right side up.

Do we expect to have faith strike us like lightning? Lightning does strike people. Faith does come in a flash—sometimes. But God has a better way. *Faith comes from what is heard, and what is heard comes by the preaching of Christ.* (Romans 10:17)

Open your Bible and begin to hear Christ speak. *Faith comes from what is heard.* The simple act of opening your Bible with expectancy is an act of faith, and in the sight of God it is a prayer that he will answer. When we begin to study the Word, our faith begins to grow *through faith for faith.*

God gave us no lids for our ears as He did for our eyes, so that we might always be open to His Word and to one another's needs.

GIVE *us this day our daily bread.* If we pray at all, it is in some today. We pray because we belong in our Father's Family. He is more ready to give us good gifts than we are to ask.

We are rooted and grounded in God's love. Our prayer is the declaration of our dependence. It is only in our foolish fancies that we are independent, self-contained and self-supporting.

What we once thought was our independence turned out to be our destruction. An independent rosebush which would uproot itself would soon wither and die. The dependent rosebush is rooted in the soil, and its dependence is its life.

We must be rooted and grounded in God's love today. Tomorrow's dependence cannot help us today. This day we must declare our dependence and pray. When we do this, the great loneliness is banished, and we are at home in God our Father.

I am the vine, you are the branches. He who abides in me, and I in him, he it is that bears much fruit, for apart from me you can do nothing. (John 15:5)

A
Wise
Passiveness

OUR hearts can go on beating for seventy years and more because there is a rest between each two beats. There is a wise passiveness. Trees and plants have their seasons of rest and activity. Our bodies have need of sleep in every circle of the sun, and we neglect this at our peril.

Our spirits need rest. *Rest in the Lord, and wait patiently for him.* (Psalm 37:7) *They that wait upon the Lord shall renew their strength.* (Isaiah 40:31)

Tiredness begins in the mind. The real root of weariness is there. Real rest begins in the soul. Our source of refreshment is in God, who comes to dwell within us and to direct us. We have a God who is alive and in our midst. The ultimate issue of all events is in His hands. *Cast all your anxieties on him, for he cares about you.* (I Peter 5:7)

We need to practice this breaking of the tension. We do it in prayer, when our praying is the response of our minds to the overwhelming goodness and glory of God. *Consequently he is able. Christ the power of God.*

Make your own selection of Bible verses which affirm the love and the power of God.

God Is Spirit

In both the Old and the New Testaments the word *spirit* is used for air in motion.

The air is a reality, invisible, mysterious, penetrating, life-giving. Sometimes gentle and caressing, again it is invading power, imperious like a storm.

The Spirit of God is like all that. He is unseen, but known. He is available to all in all our needs, and no man can monopolize Him. When we come to the end of our strength or of our folly, He is there. When sin or defeat or death shows our helplessness, He is there with His forgiveness and courage and victory.

In the majesty and loveliness of the earth, in the darkness and the terrors of judgment, He is as far away as the air we breathe, but no farther. And when we have finished the long flight from our conscience, He is there still to condemn the wrong and to maintain the right.

God is Spirit. God is invisible, invading mystery made manifest in the gentle, refreshing breeze and in the storm that topples rotting things and structures without foundations.

God is Spirit. The very air speaks to us, when we listen.

The Long View

THE doctor who takes care of my eyes tells me that our eyes are long-vision instruments. They were made for the long view. They tire from looking only at things near. They should be rested from close work by being periodically focused on the long view.

I will lift up mine eyes unto the hills. We should lift our eyes from print and figures to the horizon, or at least to the distant tower. Our power to take even the short view depends on our frequently taking the long view.

This is the strategy for convalescence. We must look at our gains; not at the end of the day, but at the end of a week. And in our soul's convalescence, which our fathers called sanctification, we judge ourselves not by the ground we have gained at the day's close, but after six months of keeping ourselves in the love of God.

When we look at the world around us, we rightly fear; but when we look up to God and get the long view we find faith. Lincoln said that he could see how a man looking down on the earth could doubt God, but not how a man looking up into the heavens could be an unbeliever. The French have this proverb: "To understand earth you must have been in heaven."

Jesus tells us about the terrors that are coming on the earth, and then He says, *Now when these things begin to take place, look up and raise your heads, because your redemption is drawing near.* (Luke 21:28)

"I⊤ ɪs by no journey of our feet that we go away from God, or return to God." Augustine told his own story in those few words—and our story.

It is a long trip that leaves our conscience behind. It is an exceeding long journey that gets us away from ourselves. It is a trip, so far away that no soul has yet made it, that outdistances God. See Psalm 139.

Jacob cashed in on his brother's weakness, and then tried to make accomplices of his heels. He laid his head down in a foreign land, and found there was a person-to-person connection with Heaven.

The prodigal went into a far country, and discovered that he did not erase the memory of his father, and that he could not dispense with his help.

God is the One who confronts us wherever we flee. And in the moment when dread of His pursuit becomes joy in His presence then we are at home.

> Halts by me that footfall:
> Is my gloom, after all,
> Shade of His hand, outstretched caressingly?
> Ah, fondest, blindest, weakest,
> I am He Whom thou seekest!
> Thou dravest love from thee, who dravest Me!

119

Waiting

Explorers in Africa tell that the natives, who were carrying the baggage, would stop every now and then in the forest path. They explained their stops, saying, "We are resting in order to let our souls catch up with our bodies."

If men, on foot in the forest and on narrow paths, feel that their bodies outrun their souls, what must happen to us on four-lane highways at eighty miles an hour? Do we find meditation and prayer and worship and kindness so difficult because we have left our souls in the garage, and our bodies are a thousand miles away?

Is there a heavenly insight in this saying of the African men? Could this be the reason why God set a day of rest at the end of six days of our bearing burdens?

And therefore will the Lord wait, that he may be gracious unto you . . . blessed are all they that wait for him. (Isaiah 30:18)

Wait on the Lord, and keep his way. (Psalm 37:34)

When to Pray

Pray whenever you feel like praying.

Pray especially when you don't feel like it, and God will help you to want to pray.

Pray when you are sad, that God will give you His gladness.

Pray when you are glad, that God will, in your gladness, make you tender toward the sad, and to save your gladness from being self-centered.

Pray when things look hopeless, because our God is *the God of hope*. (Romans 15:13)

Pray when you are poor, because our God is rich. (Ephesians 2:4)

Pray when you are rich that you may be *rich toward God*. (Luke 12:21)

Pray when you are sure that what you are asking is God's will for you.

Pray when you are not sure of the will of God; pray until He shows you His will.

Pray when you have a desire for which you dare not pray; pray that God will take that desire away.

Pray constantly. (I Thessalonians 5:17)

Prayer is the greatest guided missile in God's universe.

The
Invisible

SOME people seem to scorn the unseen as if it were unreal, and to treat the seen as alone real, living on the basis of what the eye sees and the hand can grasp. Is this sound reasoning and acting?

The truth is that the things we cannot see play a larger part in our lives than those we can see. More people trip over things they do not see than over boulders in their path. More people are made happy by love and loyalty and kindness than by gold and houses and motorcars. And more people come to grief because their spirits are warped than because their bodies are crooked.

Since the invisible plays such a great role in our lives, would we not be wise to pray for and to welcome the vision that sees the unseen?

The real battle is always in the soul. What happens to minds is more important than what happens to buildings. *For the things that are seen are transient, but the things that are unseen are eternal.* (II Corinthians 4:18)

Confess and Be Healed

WHEN we sin, we wound ourselves. *He that sinneth against me wrongeth his own soul.* (Proverbs 8:36) The wound becomes infected. It is full of "proud flesh."

How can we find healing? Confession cleanses the wound of the proud flesh. There is nothing that cuts away our pride like confessing our faults. It cleanses the wound in our own hearts, and it disinfects the wound in the heart of the person we have hurt.

But confessing only cleanses the wound. It still needs a daily dressing of prayer. It will not heal without this regular antiseptic treatment. Confess to God; confess to the person you have injured, and each pray for the other. Healing follows. It is God's surgery and medicine for our hearts when full of sores.

Therefore confess your sins to one another, and pray for one another, that you may be healed. (James 5:16)

He that covereth his sins shall not prosper: but whoso confesseth and forsaketh them shall have mercy. (Proverbs 28:13)

I said, I will confess my transgressions unto the Lord; and thou forgavest the iniquity of my sin. (Psalm 32:5)

Open
to
God

EDWIN BOOTH ran his theater behind the curtain as though it were a church. That is what Joseph Jefferson said about that great actor.

Booth once received a letter from a clergyman who said that he would like to come to Booth's theater but he was afraid some of his parishioners might object. He asked about some side or back door through which he could slip unseen.

Edwin Booth sent him this reply: "There is no door in my theater through which God cannot see." The clergyman deserved his rebuke.

The curtain has not yet been invented, nor the door built, through which God cannot see. All our work and all our play are done in the sight of God. This is what makes our work useful and enduring; and it makes our play a re-creation.

We do not want to be out of God's sight, even if it were possible. It is His presence that gives significance and joy to our life. We are glad that He sees us; and this knowledge keeps us from trying to slip into forbidden doors. This knowledge gives us courage to open the right doors. It gives to all our life the quality of worship.

Where to Pray

Is THERE any particular place where Jesus commands us to pray? Yes, He said to pray in *your room*. This meant the "strong room" in which a man kept his valuables in the days before banks were available. *Go into your room and shut the door and pray to your Father who is in secret.* (Matthew 6:6) Here are your bankbook, your stocks and bonds. Lay them out before your Father. Count them in His presence. Ask Him if they are worth what they cost you. Consider their value to you a hundred years from now. Ask Him what relation they ought to have to Him now. Pray over your checkbook, as you are praying now with your Bible open before you. Your Father is with you in *your room*.

A woman's "strong room" may be her kitchen, her dining room, her parlor. Here her treasures are gathered, and here she is to pray among them. Your Father will tell you whether you have spent too much on them and too little on the Kingdom of God. *For where your treasure is, there will your heart be also.*

The kingdom of heaven is like a merchant in search of fine pearls, who, on finding one pearl of great value, went and sold all that he had and bought it. (Matthew 13:45-46)

Competition

COMPETITION means to seek or to strive for in company with others. It is really co-operation in asking for and working toward some good. We make our petitions together and they are competition.

If we think that good things are so limited that one man's having must mean another man's lack, then competition becomes grabbing and selfish. If we think that there is plenty for all, then competition becomes the process by which we make our common demands on the resources of God's universe. If we feel that God is stingy, we try to get for ourselves. If we feel that God's plenty is sufficient for all, then we help one another to get each his share of good.

We know that God has ample supplies of forgiveness for all. When He gives me that great gift, it will not mean that my neighbor must go without it. My courage from Christ, my hope in Him, any amount of love I receive does not diminish your supply.

Our common worship is the great competition. The more I have, the more you are going to have. And the more you have of the gracious, all-glorious, cleansing, refreshing presence of God, the more I have.

Think how this applies to the production and distribution of coal and cars, and toasters and clothing, and wheat and meat. Then that will be your supplement to this short article. Right thinking and right doing could heal the sickness of an acquisitive society.

Some of God's Answers

WE PRAY for endurance, and God sends us suffering, for *suffering produces endurance.* (Romans 5:3) A woman said, "I prayed for endurance, and God sent me a blundering cook." We ask God for a particular virtue, and He sends us the raw material out of which we can make it.

We pray for obedience, and God sends us suffering. Even Christ *learned obedience through what he suffered.* (Hebrews 5:8)

We pray for unselfishness, and God gives us the opportunity to consider the feelings of others. (Philippians 2:4)

We pray for victory over temptation, and the things of the world swoop down upon us in a storm of temptation, for *this is the victory that overcomes the world, our faith.* (I John 5:4)

We pray for strength and humility, and some messenger of Satan buffets us till we lie in the dust, and hear the Lord say, *My power is made perfect in weakness.* (II Corinthians 12:9)

We pray to be drawn closer to Christ, and God lets friends turn away from us and against us.

> Man may trouble and distress me,
> 'Twill but drive me to Thy breast.

We pray for love, and God puts us among people who are unlovely. They say things that rasp our nerves. God says, "Here is your chance to show love. Here is the abysmal need of love. *Love is patient and kind.*" (I Corinthians 13:4-8)

127

A Prayer for Our World

ETERNAL God, we, who have seen, in a moment, in the twinkling of an eye, the very elements dissolve in fervent heat, and life perish in atomic blast; we, who have learned afresh that in the material world there is no security, turn now to Thee in whom alone our souls can find salvation. We put all our trust in Thee, who wast and art and evermore shalt be.

Most Merciful God, we confess that we have sought knowledge and power more than virtue and love, and so are unfit to use rightly the mastery we have won over nature. O God, in Thy compassion, grant us yet time to repent. Avert from us the consequences of folly, forbid that we should have to eat all the fruits of pride and greed and hate. Teach us how in brotherhood with all men we may make our new knowledge a blessing.

O God, whose righteousness is like the great mountains in this sinful world, give us patience and humility to endure wrong without avenging ourselves; and courage to use our strength to bring help to the helpless; and wisdom to discern the right way. And as we pray, each for himself, so we pray for the nations, that we may be kept in paths of honor, and maintain justice and freedom and peace. And to God, Father, Son and Holy Spirit be glory, world without end! Amen.